black diaries

Also by Jill Hoffman

Mink Coat (poems), Holt, Rinehart & Winston
Jilted (a novel), Simon & Schuster

Distributed by: Bernhard DeBoeur, 112 East Centre
Street, Nutely, NJ 07110, and Ubiquity Distributors, Inc.
607 Degraw St, Brooklyn, NY 11217. Available also from
Box Turtle Press.

Cover Design: Robert Steward
Cover Photograph: Clifford Singer
Book Design: Easton Davy

Copyright © 2000 by Box Turtle Press
184 Franklin Street
New York, New York 10013
212.219.9278; Mudfishmag@aol.com

ISBN: 1-893654-02-8

Mudfish Individual Poet Series No. 2

jill hoffman

black diaries

BOX TURTLE PRESS

NEW YORK

Many of the poems in this book have appeared in magazines and journals: *"Jack,"* in The New Republic; *"Mother Goose,"* and *"What King,"* in The New Yorker; *"Poem for Two Pianos,"* in Antaeus; *"Nudists," "Late August,"* and *"Regret,"* in Partisan Review; *"Terry,"* and *"The Mountain Bounder,"* in Community Review, CUNY; *"Documentary,"* and *"Rave Review,"* in Purchase Poetry Review; *"Lewiston,"* in Bennington Review; *"Dorigen," "Astrophel,"* Coca-Cola," "Greek Myth," "Myrrh," "To Robin Hood," "Cigar Band,"* and *"Amphisbæna,"* in The Bad Henry Review; *"OTB,"* in Cover; *"Sorry. I Think You Have the Wrong Number,"* and *"Puffy's,"* in Helicon Nine; *"Tar,"* in Poetry New York; *"Poem After Sir Thomas Wyatt,"* (as *"Poem"), "Black Diamond,"* and *"Sculptor,"* in Private; *"The Last, The Dulcimer, and The Broken Mermaid,"* in Now This; *"Corner Florist," "Plastron"* (as *"Box Turtle"), "Lockport Dolomite"* (as *"Mudfish"), "I am a kind of burr; I shall stick," "Star," "Worn Terrycloth,"* Urban Rape," "Vlad's Glads," "Citibank," "Prose," "Dark Sister," "Nits," "English Cut Leaf Birch," "Burdock," "Phantom Mare," "Eternity" "Oil of Primrose," "Mouse in Bottle," "You Are My Letter to Moscow," "Deadly Use," "Manhattan Community College"* (as *"Love Poem"),* and *"Marriage"* (as *"You"),* in Mudfish; *"Veteran's Day,"* in Bookstore Review; *"2 Oct,"* in The West Side Spirit; and *"The Coat,"* in The New Positivist. *"I am a kind of burr; I shall stick,"* and *"Worn Terrycloth"* are reprinted in The Second Word Thursdays Anthology (Bright Hill Press); *"Urban Rape,"* is reprinted in Roth's American Poetry Annual; and *"What King"* in Margaret Shepherd's Calligraphy Calendar.

For Renate and Dick

CONTENTS

One: *Foreskin*

Two: *Frankly,*

Three: **Cyrillic**

Four: **Burrs**

One: Foreskin

WHAT KING

What King lives in that apartment on B'way
across from me on the fifteenth floor
that all of his windows, and his only,
in a whole city should be red gold,
the sun sitting down with him under a
chandelier to stuff himself and talk
of courtesans, his travels, spring
uprisings, proposing dazzling toasts?

JACK

A few frail beans thrown overnight from a high window
onto some earth below
in disgust
because he had traded a cow for them left him dreaming
so strenuously
that his muscles ached and he could hardly lie down
again by morning
to be awakened by a mermaid from a nearby creek
combing his leafy
spinach hair, diving for pennies in the swimming light, excreting
vegetable dye from her long green tail.
His mother was aghast when she saw the giant
asparagus
that could never fit into a pot and would be too tough
to feed them;
holding on to the pink nubs like breasts in his velvet tunic
with soft leather high boots, thinking about angels
and traveller's checks
he got out the hard-boiled egg sandwich that she had thrown
into a bag for him
and climbed until he wanted only his dinner, and to eat it
in the kitchen,
never dreaming that he would meet a girl who laid golden eggs.
This girl didn't want to be told fairy tales; nobody, she said,
knew her life.
She was dressed in rags and was on a water diet, had married
the wrong man and once a month
produced a solid extra large 14 karat egg that she banged

(4)

down repeatedly on the desks of chief surgeons and the heads of hospitals
but all they could think to do was take off her breasts.
Jack carried her down the beanstalk in a sling to his mother.
And started up again.

This time the giant was waiting for him.
A gigantic egg slicer, open in the courtyard just where the top-most tip touched lawn,
stood ready to slice the boy whole for a delicious hero sandwich on Italian bread.
Only the breeze shuttling on the sharp cords made woeful harp music
like a siren in love warning Odysseus away.
And then it was he saw the giant's diminutive daughter, washing king-sized drawers
standing on a ladder bent over a raised swimming pool such as one sees in the perspiring backyards of the middle-class poor with a handle like a pail.
Half-way down the beanstalk, girdled by her consenting arms and legs, he remembered to ask the high-born girl
her name,
but when she buzzed in his ear the dizzying monosyllable famous from childhood, they fell. Jack &

Jill, Jack & Jill.
They could be seen for days, like a man in an open
elevator shaft
who had not finished a remark to his comrades. Cartwheels of surprise, surprise.
And everyone who saw them never believed in fairy tales again.

MOTHER GOOSE

Cradling her, my will grown loose as skin,
I sit with her sage head always in my lap
and my mouth full of silly verses.
Or, shaking her off like fat drops of rain
and making a run for it,
there is a shabby umbrella tucked under my wing
and a baby in my basket everywhere I waddle.

TERRY

After a life whose very
Brevity was terrific,
Your fixations remain behind
Estranged from each other
But walking around the city in your brilliant clothes
That have suffered
While their owner is so fresh, so unfaded,
I still haven't reread Tennyson's
In Memoriam which I was so dying
To read before you were dead.
I feel like an oyster growing a pearl.
(What boots it now to think of buying boots?)
I will put it under my tongue
And ferry it to you, soon.

THE LIGHTHOUSE KEEPER

(after Thoreau)

The chiffon ocean bordered by berries
The black bird with his red heart showing
The brick cylinder painted white
All the iron work painted white
Except the floor
And the dim beams that brighten thirty miles
Out to sea
That go over our heads as if in Latin aimed at the
Twin Capes of Flattery and Disappointment
So that a traveller who slept in the lighthouse would be kept
Awake all night imagining he dreams
Mainly of sailors studying him on his couch
Like Bob White whose name is an invitation.

The foghorn recites the bare end-words of a
Sestina, or on clear nights the moon slips its disc
From the revolving box, the Indian's first cache
Of sweeping glances we wreck ourselves upon
Tied to the mast like capsized figureheads.
Admiral Byrd's wife frozen on a stretcher smiles
Which is all she has time for as the virtues knell and the last
waves
Take their numbers from a machine on the counter

And wait in line, not like Hamlet and Laertes.

But we live in an ant-hill at the base of that bright phallus
And crawl in tunnels of poverty-grass to our hovel:
The woodbine of language enrolls the sand in its cause
And beyond it the sea that serves for disaster,
That great hospital where nurses press in the patient eyes of the
tossed.

POEM FOR TWO PIANOS

I wanted to write a poem in which I had a
wife
so I could say
"and my wife
leans
heavily full of child over the banister
to call my
name"
or "my wife
in our sleep bathes me
with the eaten sponge of our dreams"

only I am a married
woman
and my husband pounds his
fist
on the typewriter whenever I
mention his penis,
so that all my poems must perpetually
lie alone
in the bridal suite shunned by
columns and columns of
brides.

TAR

The battery's gone from our black hood and the rearing
white car next to it is having its parts installed
by a gang that lives on the steps of an all-night store
—strange chicken claws and spilled paella near one tire—
who shake hands with Johnny English and his dog.
Each morning he turns on the bicentennial hydrant
and a torrent meets my ankles or eyes, not without some
pleasure in a beach made entirely of black tides
for the tie-dyed sons of Neptune (mine among them),
skillful in their glistening down the flood on skateboards.
But I have seen him from the bathroom window hump
that hydrant at dawn in the act of unscrewing, red
flowers flopping in a wreath on his black brim, or stalk
like vengeance across the ford to silence a white lady.
He is roofless, he sleeps against our wall.
Like nudists you could have loved if not for their
genitals, or Arab women with veils, one is thrust
into indecent exposure; as walking past that huge building
that was gone last night we saw the windows
that had not seen light for all these years
and the immured surprised at their cobwebbed banquet.

NIGHT FEEDING

Standing in the toilet manually expressing
one drop at a time in the cracked basin
the left breast filling the john exploding
He bolted into the bathroom years ago
to find me dead
or bleeding from the wrists in a hot
tub or writing
some few words settling for pity,
but I was shaving my legs while he slept;
one Scots woman I heard of—she was a
gynecologist—
set fire to her pubic hair to shorten it, then jumped
into the tub:
        he breaks
between his tiny fingers some branch
of magic to hold
against me, the long wine-red oldest
daughter
dancing exposed in the dark fetal swirl of his thinning hair.

OTB

The place fascinated you who rode
a tired horse who did well.
I placed a hundred bets. I wove
red ribbons in his mane. I sold
my hair to buy you lunch. Our poems
made love under the waiter's eyes.
Wherever we ate, no one died there.

Now I cannot walk on Broadway.
They scan place and show and win,
lunging at trousers and crotch,
weaving, yelling, swiping
at our children who eat an idle ice cream, the day
pointless as a cap gun.

RAVE REVIEW

The brilliant confused first novels
of his lovemaking
chill me with their perversity.

At the moment of joy it is proper
for the man to become woman
and *vice versa*.

But when I say to him, "Slave,
come!" and he is charged
with amazing obedience,

I swell like Holofernes for my prize, my
Judith. When my trunk stands up,
my head lolls behind.

I see it coiffed in its new page-
boy, with the surprised porcelain look
of our son in huge waves.

NUDISTS

This anniversary of salt
we boiled out of an ocean of fire
for twelve years in a tub
as if we would not die if we did not die drowning
(and I smelled the fresh grass
in the pantries of air!)
has lain bare that you are thinking
of duty and I of
flies copulating in the pandemonium
on a beach that has known all kinds.

LATE AUGUST

Most cunning lover of herself whispering
into the boudoir of her ear

I lay you to rest in a dusty couch
and get me your sister

whose brown forehead is grooved with the tracks
of the patrolling jeep. The rocker flies off the porch:

her interrupted nights open the bureau drawers spewing
smalls
in a corner, where her friend sits who is like a bride

in a canopy bed
watching the machinations of her mourners
fornicate on her tray, with the groom

who has the mien of a butler, carrying over his arm
waves in a blizzard

when, on the last morning, all the green girls wear veils.

ROMAN À CLEF

Afraid that I'll impale you
you want me to write
out what I want, giving some

background and sketching in the plot
of one
who does not want to find himself

transmogrified, nor to be a recognizable butt:
this is the first step, you say,
and we have to go by steps.

For I could come to you in your bower where even now
I hear her replacement's straw hair rustle
and you leap with your rifle to the window in the sleeping-loft

while I unveil the monument I have made
rose-dusted with Hermione's
amazing talc,

willing, as after the funeral,
when I came to take her clothes, the pink
thorn to close like a turnstile, and let me pass.

MARRIAGE

Looking at me from between my legs like a soul
in mire to the eyes,
I can converse with the damned for the first time,
opening the vulva of my face.

POEM AFTER SIR THOMAS WYATT

"Terrific," she said cooly, the word
almost her name. Alone,
she liked to go to horror movies,
like "The Night of the Living Dead."

But once in speciäl
when she me held with her eyes
that contained one other
and her voice bravely drowning

in my boast of his love, her skin
transparent with leukemia, the lurking
beauty of Vuillard taking her back, polka-
dotting faces and panes and brick and terraces. . .

Gnarled, nothing will snap me swaying between subway and sky.

BLACK DIAMOND

My best jewels melt
in your gaze—
vile jelly.

A cockroach feeling
shadow, I dart
towards you.

I am the foreskin
you ride inside, brash
subway.

Two: *Frankly,*

1. USELESS LOVE

First he was sweeping.
She could see the room
full of her own ideas
locked against her.
She stared at the door trying to think
of something inside to say.
His voice cut her up.
Attendants came bearing wardrobes
and the whole set
rotated, so that
the silver undersides of leaves
revealed their throaty
lustre,
gliding again on the solid glass
overhung by crystal fruit
to the immersed marble stairs
where the boat thuds.

2. PHARAOH

The shaky drawing of your lips
is as the bow from which the arrow flew

and my brown kisses on your neck
are concealed among bulrushes.

3. MYRRH

Your speech sums up
in lightning bolts
the patient sheaves.
There are some forty odd of them.
All of them lie down in submission to you.
All of them bow from the waist
to signify not authority
that they recognize in your motley, your Good
Year cap, or ebbing wiry hair, but a day
made up of heavenly parables
and a night of frankincense.

4. GARGOYLE

A little truck on the windowsill
captures B'way.
The plane
you see things on – your transparent tears
(invisible as your sperm)

invisible to me for months, maybe
years,
behind your golden stained mortal hand

as you lay napping during my beauty's siege.
Another Halloween leers from a pumpkin.
When you stick out your
tongue at me
I dissolve in the Hudson wearing your rainbow.

5. THE MOUNTAIN BOUNDER

You have weighed your suffering
against mine and mine
on the blindfolded lady's scale
touches the top of the lawyer's desk.
You are coy. You propose to be hard-to-get.
I have not even gotten to celebrate
your fingertip. But I will think this week
a rooftop I step over with gigantic boots,
a grey moor only, among many
in the sky, and continue
downtown towards you.

6. DOCUMENTARY

The jackal at one end of a huge meadow
calls to her mate and he answers.
They meet. She greets him
in the submissive posture,

as I greet you, still in the shade of the woods,
on my back, calling, waiting.
I have made a friend of the sky.
And my belly knows every wind.

7. THIRD RAIL

Another birthday is frankly
approaching. Last year
your face between the subway bars
making a face
as I went down the stairs, was grace.
The months turned hot
around my neck, so many
electric chairs
charming with their staying power:
old December, where is our platform
bed?

8. JEWELLED CAGE

It is noon. Midnight.
I am with you
downstairs, working
in your mysterious way
containing
me
as I plunge and thrash
my scented plumage
against your ribs,
wanting to be human.

9. AMPHISBÆNA

Together we were
a fabled serpent
able to go in both directions.
Hearing your voice, the past
opens like the Skeat's you gave me
to the etymology of everything.
I made the error
of turning my back on you.
I made the error
of turning him down.
The New Year looks both ways
before crossing
itself in joy, before crossing
the dangerous world
where love is, but can so seldom be found.
Abby, something fabulous
is happening to me.

10. SUNDAY

Calling you just now the empty ring
created floorboards. Breath. You walked,
almost answering. My heart pounded.
In all other ways, I have no imagination.

On the harmonica of my secret voice,
I call for you and wail and revel,
my cheeks bunched in bliss while my heart
travels back and forth in its cage.

11. DORIGEN

Again you are not there. Earl
laughs. I gather all the stones
from the seashore. I spend
the day stoned. The broken
date a silken cord,
I hop about at your feet
and watch the cat who watches me.
I have your word.
It is a crumb.
It is a feast.

12. TO ROBIN HOOD

What happens to me in your glance
when all those Cupids rise up against me
and release their catholic arrows

(the way as a child I imagined archers rising from the toilet
bowl when I flushed
and turned my back,
running)

this slow swooning, stuck
up, in the dark forest
of your majesty

seems light as Chaucer's purse
or as my own private
mink drawstring pouch, frankly swollen and begging for you.

13. CIGAR BAND

The men in my past
that you name
with wicked glee

entangle me less than your wild iron curls.
You hiss their names.
You are all men.

I worship the ring of sweat
on your holy flannel shirt
covered with wild geese.

14. THIS CHRISTMAS

I have seen the hiatus
of the weekend
spread until it became the Red Sea.
Then, at your sandpaper voice, it parts.

When I get to you it is fairy land.
Frank phantasies scribble the beams, the
arches, the swivel throne, the glistering floor.
What stuff I smear on my eyelids to hie me there!

Or wait at home entwined in wire net
like a sad tree cut down
in the great forest
to be hung with your star.

15. ASTROPHEL

The diurnal
hope of seeing
him that begets
diurnal disappointment

beheads the morning.
Only grass helps.
I am no queen in the tower
writing letters.

And yet I know
this kneeling on bare knees
among West End rooftops in phoenix India is the desert
of my deserving and my rich dessert.

16. GREEK MYTH

My innocence you think is bliss.
I crawl into my daughter's bed
and sob piercingly into her pierced ear
and cling prickling against her velvet skin
next to Purple Pillow.

I hated it in the drugstore
when I saw all the tempting boxes
full of condoms with reservoir tips, lubricated, hand-
rolled, that you could have used.
I had to stand there a long time with cramps and severed tubes.
And the sight of one in a blue bunting – poking its
heavenly tongue in and out –

But, O my Frank, punish me
for my over-frankness
by hand, in person, with anything
but this awful silence, this being
everywhere and nowhere.

17. "I AM A KIND OF BURR; I SHALL STICK."

(Lucio, *Measure for Measure*)

I say this to myself and fall asleep
wandering through fields of various endearments
of yours that astonish with their insensate
candor, painted on both sides.
I am not next to the pleasant obedient
husband I have given up, Helen,
whose trousers were a mother and father to me.
I am worn on the sleeve of your brutal
jacket, near the cuff.

You pretended to agree with me
when I was wrong about the meaning of 'epicene,'
showing off
your love.

But I reach up
in the house next to the lighthouse in North Truro
at the kitchen sink looking out the back
lined with purple and gold deadly wolf's bane
at the silver bay, the lacquered
golf course and bushes and historical museum
which I don't see because it is night
and raining and dangerous on the ceiling.
But I reach up and touch

the bulb and its attractive metal string.
At once it is apparent to my whole body from my thrilled fingertips.
All is changed
to this charged permanence.

18. STAR

Abby, surely this is it.
That he is not against me
without being with me
at the same time.
To him I am Hitler
with all the charms of Hitler.

If he among the clouds wishes to disappear
into the divine blur and burning
of his mysterious personality, it is the prerogative of heaven,
– of the Jewish heaven in particular.
It is part of his great work to dazzle.

But once I caught him.
With a bit of tinsel, with my daughter's
actress voice, with the glittery name, 'Susan Strasberg,'
then he came to the phone.
In a twinkling I heard his radiant voice.
I drank its cordial.

19. COCA-COLA

I am something you have bent
into an almost articulate
calligraphy grandly undressing across the sky,

transfixed by your absence-presence
against the grid
like Blake's happy widow singing her husband's song.

Three: Cyrillic

CORNER FLORIST

At night the trees disappear
where they have come from.
An occasional rollerskater strolls by
in miniature or an Egyptian
worshipper amid toy traffic riding a tiny platform,
the size of Indians surrounding cardboard forts,

while I play cards with one, who, sick with stomach virus,
enchants the stubborn minutes with his beauty.

The fraught procession across the crumbling fresco. . .
And if there is something that you cannot say
though a great veil is lifted
crosstown to Fifth Avenue over the nude body
of Central Park,
it is this: that the trees are a strange species,
wearing their mistress' clothes and scrubbing the splintery heavens.

The bourgeois reality of your hips
black lace over imagined breasts
that redhead your cock her
true self, Rachel, at last
after these fourteen hard years/

I remember my lost friends.

REGRET

Mother, when I dress him
as a woman I love him.
I wish I hadn't thrown away
some of your old girdles.

WORN TERRYCLOTH

"All but disappeared," or "The Disappeared Marriage."
Titles suggest themselves like charming prostitutes.
What I thought was something he said or thought
But it has slipped away now, one of his old slippers,
A bathrobe his daughter wears who lives with him
Though it is literally 'all holes.'
The one I like and linger on is "Mr. Rumple
And Mrs. Rumple," from something she said: "Well, I
Guess I'll go call Mr. Rumple now," as she sauntered
Straight to the phone the minute she came in.
The nights go on arguing like this, waiting for the definite
Date, the climactic 'See you in court!' to sue and be sued.

A marsupial, I hold the telephone's umbilical cord
And dangle it angrily while suddenly she goes soft
In the center, like candy. She is sad, pouting: "I drew
A little heart on the bottom of my nightgown for Valentine's
Day, and Dad won't let me color it in – "
—Some aggravating syrup in her voice—
– "On everything else when *he* does the laundry" –
The many creases that I powdered, the strong red,
The wiry diadem that later I glimpsed
Glancing into her small room that morning
When she stood suspended in front of the mirror, naked
Wearing my pearls, her red lips pursed, her eyes black diaries.

PROSE

To write it is to give it up
like vomiting
which I did one night
arms around the base of the toilet bowl.

You know you are going to pay the price.
It's just a question of how much
and maybe when.
Echoes adhere to everything and make us humble,

the dagger upheld against the breast,
remembering
who said what when.
This prose commitment to daily life, to describing

what he was like in bed
and moving over and turning
over over and over
till he is gone, and it is you.

There is even a little dog
and a bench and a garden,
I am playing a mandolin, he proffers flowers,
the whole Meissen arbor

guarded by chicken wire
and razor-ribboned around,
with a tiny gold

padlock

that only a change of
attitude can open,
like a can of worms
that turns to gold.

TARGET

In an equipoise of firmness and indifference
your member
follows me

but another shoots up like an arrow and pierces my heart.

LEWISTON

All my complaints gather
like artists dividing space in a gallery

your courtesy is so serious
in the supermarket, green brown
eyes rivering down on me in a whirlpool

even the red is courteous
and passionate
in the Russian whites of your eyes

your hands and feet are Cyrillic
your hair weeps sweat

this love that takes me by surprise like a band of men
who tied me to the ground in their brown suits
when I went through the mail chute to their arms

makes me whimper
with joy
like a bitch

SCULPTOR

The boulders of your stare above your cheekbones
— the tray in my hands —
pinned me in the air above the table

like Christ caught worshipping Magdalene
or a woman in a meadow whose blossoms dishevel with dew.

PLASTRON

She has come out of her shell a little
on the gold Bokhara, her neck
stretched out and bowed, dragging towards the carpet
like Anne Boleyn on *her* bronze morning
among the huge ravens in the Tower courtyard.
As soon as we brought her here
the male humped her.
Perhaps her daughter will be queen.
Most assuredly she will live with her father as his wife,
wearing a cocktail waitress' uniform
while he services her
on his hands and knees at her high heels.
Her one sick eye is closed as if better.
The pet man says she is fifteen.
He stretched his neck across her phoenix back
and his orange arms and legs hung down
over her but she hid.
Her dotty head has yellow spots,
and her arms flutter weakly with their long fingernails like a typist's.
You are absent from me in coldness of mind
camouflaged I see
as the bureau's sun-mottled leg, so cleverly
in the deep recesses of my bedroom
that you are the Trojan horse and I am Helen.
My daughter has written a libretto to herself,
a teenager in the mirror, inspired by the
popular song, 'I will survive,'
and she sings it to me on the telephone.

JACK TAR

There is a porthole
through which I am able perfectly well to see you
in three places, mowing the lawn, pouring a concrete
patio, and the third activity is more
dangerous and ephemeral, saying hello to someone?
I believe you are an angel
but that brings it all so close to heaven I complain.
Young man, bringer of provisions, ship's
chandler, Antony,
you puff out your cheeks and leap by sheer exertion
in through the rotting sash of my bathroom window
on the fifteenth floor where I am petrified.
Bright colors have been discovered under the dark varnish.
The virgin Mary on a blue cloud holding a sparkling
shroud, but the icon under the icon remains
like some unalterable truth with Russian overtones,
like love, although the paint is thin and flayed.

MANHATTAN COMMUNITY COLLEGE

In my stories before the bell
the I think Japanese man who claims the seat
by inserting his briefcase in an almost sexual
way, then squeezing in, takes out his long blue
cigarettes (it is obscene that they are not joints),
taps on the packet, lights one, then
gets out his disgusting brush. His hair is braided
in spidery chains leaving bald stretches.
At this I rise, and he says, "Look
lady, there is shit on your dress. See."
Standing till 59th Street I had looked down
on the eyelids (faint blue), the spidery lashes
of eyes protuberant like mine. No chin.
The face ending in the bottom lip. Red stockings,
white slacks with cummerbund, red blouse, black
skin. This thin girl in her pert Christmas way
before the door could close
had a cop knocking at the window at his braided head
and the man out on the platform at the end of a long
                                          nightstick.
So I come to you, — but Yvrose is like a red rose
in a white eyelet blouse, cheeks incarnadine, the roster
aglow with Daffodil, Altagracia, Daisy Rivera, Maria deJesus.

DOGWOOD

Don't try to sound like a poem
whatever you do
sound like a hyena rather

waking up in the morning with a good howl
at the scent of your mate,
carnivorous, beside you,

who has been out all night
painting a house white in Lakewood, New Jersey,
whose huge nostrils
bring lilacs.

STUART AT BENNINGTON

The children are the way you feel
about Debbie you say, the smell
of both of you together. It is
this smell that children are born for,
their scalps, heaven.

The honk of Max, brother of Jonathan.
Chauncey panting all around not knowing
what she wants, like her owner they said.
You doing pushups like monumental sculpture.

And the grass that is "not a nutrient"
like July girls, fireflies, tempting us into
secret gardens, groves of Comus and the Fair Lady
that have graduated, still alive!
We move like mountains groping after those fey lanterns.

LOCKPORT DOLOMITE

I am a broom that the Shakers made.
I must sweep the screened rooftops with my hair,
everything wearing its hardware cloth mantle like Miss Havisham.
You found me in a dresden clock with my crumpled bill of sale.
You like old stuff, antiques; prying loose old nails.
Never could I say enough about your shoulders
even if I should walk out to the edge of some escarpment, and jum

VETERAN'S DAY

It is twilight all day today
and grouchy moods twitch hypothetically
like rain in dark gutters.
This is harmony, or whatever you call it.
Together, we can forget each other.
And go about our real business.
When I smile on Canal Street
it is because of your dark word
from smiling lips
that entered me with an amorous thrust.
You said to be careful
because the night before last in the rain
a truckdriver absolutely didn't see me
wearing black on the black street.
I said 'no' and you hunched a little
as if with pain in the hall and left again.
Our quarrel like a wall of names.

MOUSE IN BOTTLE

The small brown beer bottle
contains a mouse
whose eyes are pointing at me,
as in the old game for embarrassed kissing.
Her face is like the vegetables
that hardened in my mother's fridge
after her death, grey husks almost beautiful.
When she scurried about
and made ready to leave
the nest to forage for her next
meal, and go towards life, and stay longer at the Fair,
she found she could not pass through.
My personal affairs are wrapped up in this somehow
as the cotton lumps fall and it is hard to tell
where fur ends and the soul begins.
This bottle was found in an old garage.
This bottle was thrown by an old drunk
who wanted to murder the old woman who lived in the house
but didn't dare.
This mouse was attracted by the brown glass dwelling
as the moon is attracted to the buttocks of certain men.
The collection of fuzz is so valuable
I want to smash the bottle to roll in it.

URBAN RAPE

You are sleeping in a tent near the woods
exactly where we found box turtle and nine months later
let him go again.
Today I bought you a size larger.

The names we have called each other
drag around the living room resting on tar
sculptures that are living roads,

as he did, dying, for sun and a female.
Only the parakeets
make love to their caged moments with unthreatened song.

The plants are demanding vodka.
Then
I am lying spread-eagled in a clearing bleeding money.

2 OCT

Laundry. Recipes. Mice. My daughter
is away and my mind begins to fill
the house. Unbelievable. I am happy.
The day is the same color as my top
which I machine-washed without ruining.
Pale silvery grey. The artist I live with
likes older women and the way my left
fist curls when I walk down the street.
Maybe someday I will feel again like "It,"

the concubine who has ensnared the love of the maharaja.
His paintings of the sleeping gypsy and the lion
describe the calm when my children are sleeping.
At dawn we swim in the pool of the college that fired me.
I wear my hair unbraided so that he will not pull it.

"SORRY. I THINK YOU HAVE THE WRONG NUMBER."

Goddess, help me to see
the glamour
of the life that I've got
I said as a Russian
prince left my red chamber
penniless
and my shorter and shorter
lines wanted to be novels.
I look for my reading glasses.
And you who have everything
don't seem to mind
the loss of muse
as I the loss of paradise
and have bright things to say all over
so that the sky is a mural of your voice.

VLAD'S GLADS

The tall gladiolas
bent
and dangled towards
the glass table

their pursed fuchsia
lips. Still the withered
crones could be plucked,
the young girls left.

But now they are all
in a lowly
carafe, mature
women not minding death.

THE RED AND THE BLACK

Everything is math. My weak
subject. I go into Bloomingdale's
to try on the Chanel Red Lipstick
and then in to the sinus doctor to hold the black
bowl and bow my head over it.

At night in bed I am adding up
what you cost me. The list
covers pages tacked up in the
kitchen. I don't come.
Once again, I have gotten the wrong answer.

THE LAST, THE DULCIMER, AND THE BROKEN MERMAID

We are still recovering from Carolyn's visit.
Some drenching hurricane, named Hugo,
was shaking our perimeters
when she arrived, a world traveller.
Her Japanese boyfriend with the name of a camera
is put away like a folded parasol
and she is breathing
easier now and deeply and looking up and around at everything.
I remembered all her advice to me –
"I love the way men like to hedge their bets. . . Close
that account; close that account or it will bankrupt you!"

She has a truck; her destination is vague: the Carolinas.
She had been raped in New Orleans and stabbed in the lungs.
She had been run over by a car. On the way back from Costa Rica
where she went to recover, the plane crashed. Worst of all,
she was burned out from teaching Freshman English.

This is how it started. She called from Amherst,
where she was visiting a friend. And I said, Sure, stop by.
I didn't know she was homeless; that Ni Kong
had just told her he was "seeing someone else."
Her truck was an open van with all her possessions
loose, that had to be carried inside piece by piece.
She was like Blanche, seeking shelter.
It doesn't matter whether she wanted to destroy us.
Her voice was Hiroshima. "Listen, you guys. . ."

in a southern, nasal, annihilating accent. Kali,
she waved her arms for exercise in the living room.
My worst fear was that she would overhear me on the telephone
(this house has unpredictable acoustics, like a beach).

Her skin looked like a baby's though she smoked.
That was because she had a chemical burn, she said.
All the top skin of her face had been removed.
I let her read a few pages of my novel.
After that, she said she had bad news and good news.
The bad news was the main character was unbelievably naive.
What's the good news, Carolyn, I said. The good news was
she had an idea that I shouldn't write a novel at all
but a screenplay. Write dialogue. Make money.
And she started helping me map out the movie.
When my friends came she put on a grey wool hat
and covered all her hair like a concentration camp victim
and wouldn't let me tell them the idea.
You and she agreed politically: the Palestinians, those
shadow-Jews. . . Even my daughter respected her opinions.
At night in the bedroom I whispered, "She's my mother."

You were shaking. Evenings, she opened the bedroom door
and lay down next to you on the bed. "She's your
friend," I accused. "Well, she's an acquaintance,
but not my relative," you answered.
Ni Kong was twenty when she met him; she was forty.
That was six years ago. When she had stayed with us once
before, she had been an excellent cook.
"I could never cook for that man," she said.
I said she could stay until the weekend.
You said she could stay until Monday morning.

(67)

She went into the little room like Hitler's bunker
and started reading my daughter's Nancy Drew books.

On the seventh day I gave her the Chinese doll
I bought at dawn in London that looked like my mother
dying. My mother had given it back to me,
but was pleased when I told her my maid said
it looked like it was about to come to life.
When she was leaving, it was clear
there would be no fond postcard from the road.
"Oh, I never write to anyone," she said.

The day she left I was moving law books for my father,
Bender's *Forms of Pleading.* You stayed to see it through.
Afterwards, you wanted to do a sculpture entitled
"Woman." Just a long skinny pipe, leaking at the top.
Instead, we paired a rusty shoemaker's last, and the dulcimer
Carolyn gave you. "It needs a third element," you said,
and on the jutting foot like a lonely rock sticking up into the sky,
you placed the broken mermaid, with her clay tail broken off,
singing of Carolyn's visit.

PUFFY'S

I stood at the window on the street
in a new red jacket, linen, with wide shoulders.
A lady sat next to you at the bar.
A man and a woman at a table were distracted
by my serious expression. The man motioned towards you
and mouthed "him?" I put my finger to my lips.
She turned around, I winked. Wife alert, wife alert, wife
alert he said as I watched your back in the plaid flannel shirt
I bought at Syms. I didn't hear a word he said. Slowly
you turned around, and smiled, an alcoholic.

Four: Burrs

DARK SISTER

for Wendy

Dark sister, always in my
shadow, disadvantaged
in years

my first sexual partner
with whom the boredom of being a prisoner
was shared

little, brown, compliant, willing,
we took turns
being the boy. The boy touched

the girl. The night I remember
Dad came in. A wedge of light in our bedroom like God
angry in Paradise.

I had taken off my pajama bottoms
but left on my pajama tops.
"Go to sleep," he said gruffly, unsuspecting.

I was under my own covers with my long sleeves showing!
Now your lawyer calls me from Vermont,
a specialist in child abuse and molestation.

We lied for each other every day
and swore we practised twenty minutes.

(73)

Dad protected you against Mother.

We ate at separate tables, we were vegetarians,
you ate meat.
You told the neighbors you had a 'muzen brothers.'

In the bath, Dad taught you all the states and capitals.
I never learned them.
You called Gregory Peck Geography Peak.

Later, you said, "I only feel
happy when I have a Slinky
between my legs."

Next you are at a seminar in Boston, Female
Victims of Incest. Suddenly, I am in the same
shoes as our grandfather, who molested us.

I feel like some man who has gotten some lady pregnant.
You remember that one day we gave each other
a very dirty look, and I went off

to Emily Tendler's house for some reason
and left you alone
for him to do his number on you.

I remember
my shock when you told
that it wasn't only me,

the fairer one.
"I'm in analysis!" you hiss. We must sell the jewels.

Then Dad is served with a summons in his office.

This is your latest 'dance.'
First, writhing on the couch, then
sharpening your knife on our father's testicles.

Finally, you are taking action
against your father,
suing him for rape, also his rich brother.

DEADLY USE

"She that herself will sliver and disbranch
From her material sap, perforce must wither
And come to deadly use."

Lear, 2.iv.40-42

We are wearing matching dresses.
You are looking at me slyly.
A tiny monkey, a used-up tramp.

Our grandfather sits behind us looking down
on my coiled braids, smirking shoulders, gangly legs
beside all the other cousins in the photograph

(*he* looks, suspiciously, handsome and sensual),
beside Linda and Susan and Paul. I am a pleased
courtesan, you frown. Your middle name is 'Sue'

and mine is 'Joy.' Forty years later,
you sue your own father, unzip your fly
and pull out your bludgeoning instrument.

I wring my bruised hands.
With wringing, my right hand
has bruised my left, my left bruises my right.

NITS

We used to curl our lip at each other
each making an ugly sneer
presided over by Queen Rotten, our mother.

What a drag you were when she died,
flying in from Chicago,
and asking her why she never loved you.

The stench was unbearable. I used to
cry out on the streets going crosstown
and smelled it in the lobby.

Only she did not smell it.
Once, saying goodbye, my hair brushed
her cheek when I bent over the bed to kiss her.

She was afraid she had caught nits
(the children had them from school).
"But my hair didn't touch you," I said.

"Yes, it did," she cried. "I know
because I thought how sweet
it felt on my cheek."

Talk of kerosene rags,
disgrace
and an ivory comb.

You, Medusa,
suing our father
in his 77th year.

ENGLISH CUT LEAF BIRCH

Evelyn, how romantic it was
making up, it was almost as if
nothing mattered but us, your voice
and mine gold snakes coupling
on a dresser top littered with
the past like sprinklings of
pot, and roaches our young
writhing, writing, white
birches

ETERNITY

"Esther's father died," my father told me.
I had one foot out the door on the way to the movies.
Esther is his wife, forty years
younger than he is, and extremely nice.
"They have no place to bury him," he added.
"Do you mind if they put him in our plot?"
Her father was younger than my father.
"Of course not!" I said, so glad in my grief
it was her father and not my father.
I went to the Village and saw *Crimes and Misdemeanors*.

Then my mother rose up against me.
Where she was buried, she sat up and she said
"What right have you to disturb my hard-earned rest?"
(she has been gone eleven years),
"to bring that woman's father here
who took away your father from me
when I was in pain and wanted him
and cried like a baby
and now this is eternity that you
know nothing about, and can never
undo, or atone for, never."
She was bringing me hot washcloths for my head
(I had a splitting headache).

The backyard looks like hell,
the wisteria in a taut line tied to a cable wire
two storeys up

that we thought was evergreen is not.
The rhododendron is a shrivelled corpse
whose ruined fingers rake the past.
Everything is suffering
this December 4th.
I remember she said Woody Allen was surely
the eighth wonder of our age.

I got so sick, I called my father finally
in Brooklyn, they were sitting shivah, and he drove
to my house and doubleparked the rented Cadillac
and rang the bell with a "chart" he called it
in his shaking hand – it was a few initials, M, B,
on the back of a shopping list – I read the
items jealously through my mother's eyes – bread,
milk, a word I couldn't make out – Was he really
living with someone else? – to show me there were two
distinct plots. Was there room for all of us? I asked.
"Of course," he answered in his unctuous lawyer's voice.

My mother always liked the cemetery. Her parents
Max and Bella have an open book at their feet.
But when she saw a spelling mistake for which
I think a sister was responsible, no, the engraver,
she said, "There was the country, the fresh air,
the schnapps, but I felt no peace. . . ."
On death's stone page is cut my undying error.
Sleep, Mama. Let these tears
be the pearly stone to mark my visit,
and the path to lead me to you on my knees.

BURDOCK

I have made a life out of burrs;
like a dead dog flung on the road's shoulder
as if asleep, or asleep with a pup nuzzling under it, that
you sculpted with bare hands and one tattered glove
suddenly both alive,
green and brown stars nappy with dead leaves

my joblessness mornings
my children gone, my lost period
a phantom mare
while the building vacates

It started to stink like a haystack
—we carried it down on a piece of burlap—
these habits stick to me like love
Afterwards the artist himself was made of invisible needles.
If a democrat wins my father will be happy.

how will we eat
this postmodernist fruit
—all its prickles hooks—
of your adamant labour?

PHANTOM MARE

A year later she comes back to me
like the ghost of my mother on *Yom Kippur*:

A phantom mare
rigged in a palatial space.

How did the beautiful soaked
braless girl in a t-shirt say
the stallions were aroused?

(We had met them in their stalls like hotel rooms.)

It is raining on the Morgan
Horse Farm — my knee is hurt, my sandals
are too thin —

and she tells us how the semen
is collected. I forget the rest.

Only one summer later
wrapped in grey rags, she gallops
back

while you are in my arms
and I am

bound, speechless

mummified with darkness
and the stained gauze of kings.

THE COAT

She rushes out with her hair wet
with the belt pulled tight
on our iridescent wool-lined trenchcoat
(we have only one coat between us)
— she is tired, she fell down the stairs at work
and turned two somersaults and everyone screamed
in slow motion
and so many images flashed in her head
like the dog who fell down the cliff in North Truro
and keeping her head tucked in gym
that she thought she was dead,
but still she has put vermilion powder on her lips —
and I remember my galvanized
rendezvous, so long ago — while she watched,
a cherub, from behind — my gilded eyes
seeking my eyes in the gilded mirror one last time.

YOU ARE MY LETTER TO MOSCOW

Tall boy with pointy chin
are your ear flaps down?
I was thrilled that your 6 ft.
duffel bags arrived safely
and even to learn that
the jam and honey jars
exploded inside ziplock bags.
My scalp felt chills
and I hated that woman
on the phone, like a corrections
officer, who kept half-
interrupting (my transatlantic
echo). I dreamed you came home
while I slept, I hugged
your long body like
an ironing board
and heard your heart
beating while I sobbed
why? why? why? on my knees.
Then I said, thinking I might be
crazy, Vladimir, do you see
Matthew?

OIL OF PRIMROSE

You have gone
to the cold house
and left me here,
my changes
matching the world's,
hot flashes
from Germany, Panama,
Romania

What an interesting
time
I cool off in the garden

Last night on television
Archbishop Desmond Tutu
in Jerusalem
said the Jews
can't (in a beautiful English accent)
can't do this, it's too horrific
the Jews
who have suffered so much
from injustice can't
make others
suffer so much.

Black messenger
from God.
                    All eyes on

the Gaza strip

Today, Matthew is 18.
Born on Boxing Day,
the day after Christmas
when you give again
what you have gotten
— it feels like yesterday!
I was at the Thalia
seeing *War & Peace*. My sister
was babysitting, deranged
but we didn't know it then.

The stethoscope
on a moving mound, I heard
a herd of wild horses gallop.
He was too beautiful for this world,
Adeline said. We scalded him
in scalding water
because he didn't make a sound.
(His sister told him he was found
outside the door in a paper bag.)

His tongue is still
heart-shaped. Last night after dinner
he argued for the legalization
of drugs, so tall, handsome

and drug-free.
He is so grown up
he doesn't hate me
when I call him by your name.
(Wrong! He still does.)

If only you had left
your good pants
so I could wash them.

The flames an invisible
intifada

      *

Like inspiration
and the long cool after

or love
that goes away

like the shadow of love
that comes back to plague you

I am burning, Israel, burning.

CITIBANK

My personal identity code your name
I slide the thin card
into the slot and money comes out
as once you held me from behind
and touched me with your hand.

Jill Hoffman is the author of *Jilted*, a novel (Simon and Schuster), 1993; and *Mink Coat*, poems (Holt, Rinehart & Winston), 1973. She was awarded a Guggenheim Fellowship in poetry and holds degrees from Bennington and Columbia, and a Ph. D. from Cornell. She teaches a writing workshop in TriBeca, and has just completed a second novel. She is the founding editor of *Mudfish*.

Mudfish Individual Poet Series

No. 1. David Lawrence, *Dementia Pugilistica*

No. 2. Jill Hoffman, *Black Diaries*

No. 3. Doug Dorph, *Too Too Flesh*

Box Turtle Press
184 Franklin Street
New York, New York 10013
212.219.9278
Mudfishmag@aol.com